Barrier-Free Travel

The Grand Canyon for Wheelers and Slow Walkers

CANDY B. HARRINGTON

Photographs
Charles Pannell

C & C Creative Concepts

To Charles

Contents

Preface — A Canyon for Everyone

At first glance, the Grand Canyon doesn't appear to be the best choice for wheelchair-users and slow walkers. And to be honest, the iconic mule ride down to the bottom of the canyon isn't. The good news is, you'll get the best views of this popular natural wonder from the rim, which boasts a nice collection of accessible trails, attractions, restaurants and lodging options. And this guide tells you about all of those, and gives you the resources to plan your own accessible getaway to the Grand Canyon.

But this guide covers more than just the popular South Rim. It also includes information on accessible attractions and lodging options on the more remote North Rim; as well as accessible sites and viewpoints along Desert View Drive, which can be accessed from the east park entrance.

And since the Grand Canyon experience extends well beyond the official boundaries of the national park, this guide also gives you information about how to access those sites and attractions. From the Grand Canyon Skywalk on the West Rim, to the only accessible way to get to the canyon floor, near Peach Springs, there's no shortage of off-the-beaten-path vacation ideas on the tribal land that borders the park. Even better, this guide also covers accessible lodging options on that tribal land.

And last but not least, there's the Grand Canyon Railway. This guide also includes access information on this historic railway that runs from Williams to the South Rim of the Grand Canyon. And if you'd like to spend a night or two in Williams before or after your journey, there's also information about accessible lodging choices there.

Although access information is good, I believe my readers are entitled to updated, accurate access information; so much so, that I made a last minute pre-press return trip to the South Rim, when I discovered my notes conflicted with some of the official access information routinely disseminated to visitors. As it turned out, my notes were correct, but I just couldn't let this book go to press if there was one iota of doubt about the accuracy of the access information.

In the end, there are many accessible ways to enjoy the Grand Canyon, and this guide presents a world of options to do exactly that. But this guide isn't just for wheelchair-users and slow walkers. Parents pushing strollers will also appreciate the accessible trails, attractions and drives in this guide. So if you just need to sit down and rest a lot, have little ones in tow, or use a walker, wheelchair or scooter, rest assured, the Grand Canyon is a great vacation choice for you. Despite its massive proportion, it really is a canyon for everyone.

Enjoy!

And if you'd like more accessible travel ideas, be sure to cruise on by my Barrier-Free Travels blog at www.barrierfreetravels.com.

Candy Harrington
www.CandyHarrington.com
Facebook: Candy Harrington
Twitter: Candy B. Harrington
Pinterest: Candy Harrington

Saint George

Mesquite

North Las Vegas

Las Vegas

Boulder City

Grand Canyon West
Page 65

Diamond Bar Road

Buck and Doe Roa

Pierce Ferry
Road

Peach Sprin
Page 77

Kingman

Lake Havasu City

89

89

Kanab

89A

67

89

160

North Rim
Page 59

Desert View
Drive
Page 43

South Rim
Page 5

64

64

Williams

89

40

Flagstaff

Grand Canyon
Railway
Page 51

Winslo

Admission and Park Passes

Admission to Grand Canyon National Park is $25 per car, and it's good for seven days. The fee is collected at the north, south and east park entrance stations, and it is good for all areas of the national park. Payment can be made with cash or a credit card. Save your receipt as you'll need to show it when you enter the park through a different gate, or if you come and go from the park. Park admission is included on all Grand Canyon Railway tickets.

A variety of national park passes are also available at the north, south and east entrance stations. They are valid at all national parks and wildlife refuges. They are not valid at Grand Canyon West or for the drive down into the canyon, as these sites are located on Hualapai tribal land, and separate entrance fees apply. Here's a list of some of the discount passes available. See if you qualify for one, as it may help trim your travel budget.

Access Pass

This free lifetime pass is available to U.S. citizens or residents with a permanent disability. Applicants must provide documentation of a permanent disability, and prove residency or citizenship. The pass also offers a 50% discount on camping and boat launching fees. It generally does not provide for a discount on fees charged by concessionaires.

Military Pass

A free annual military pass is available to active members of the Army, Navy, Air Force, Marines and Coast Guard. Reserve and National Guard Members are also eligible. Documentation required includes a Common Access Card or Military ID (Form 1173).

Senior Pass

This lifetime pass is available to U.S citizens or permanent residents age 62 or older. The cost for the pass is $10. Proof of age, and residency or citizenship are required. The pass also offers a 50% discount on camping and boat launching fees. It generally does not provide for a discount on fees charged by concessionaires.

Annual Pass

If you plan on visiting a number of national parks throughout the year, the Annual Pass may be a good deal for you. This non-transferable pass costs $80 and it's good for the entire year. It's an especially attractive deal if you live near a national park, or are planning a road trip that includes a number of national parks. You can also order this pass by calling (888) 275-8747.

South Rim

Located just 60 miles north of Williams on Highway 64, the South Rim of the Grand Canyon includes Grand Canyon Village, one of the most touristed sections of the park. On the plus side, it also offers a large selection of accessible lodging options, several accessible trails, and an accessible shuttle bus that stops at all the popular sites. And although the park concessionaires have been around since well before the Americans with Disabilities Act, they've consistently made access improvements and upgrades over the years. Thanks to these improvements, not only is the South Rim a must-do for first-time visitors, but it's also an excellent choice for wheelchair-users and slow walkers.

The Basics

Shuttle Buses

Although personal vehicles are permitted on many of the South Rim roads, a free shuttle bus system is also available. During peak times, the park gets quite crowded, and with limited parking at some of the popular sites and trailheads, it just makes sense to take the shuttle

Accessible shuttle buses transport visitors along the South Rim

bus. The shuttle buses are equipped with ramps and they can kneel to accommodate people who use assistive devices; however they cannot accommodate wheelchairs larger than 30 inches wide or 48 inches long. They also can't accommodate most scooters.

There are some stops that are not accessible, but the shuttle bus drivers are very good about suggesting alternate stops if they see a wheelchair or other assistive device. If you disability isn't obvious, and you cannot do stairs, it's a good idea to check with the driver and find out the most accessible way to get to your destination.

There are three shuttle bus routes along the South Rim: the Village Route, Hermits Rest Route and the Kaibab Rim Route. The Village Route shuttle stops at the visitor center, the campgrounds and the South Rim hotels, and operates from 5:00 a.m. to 9:30 p.m. It takes 50 minutes to complete the entire loop. The Kaibab Rim Route shuttle stops at the visitor center, Mather Point, the Yavapai Geology Museum, Yaki Point and South Kaibab Trailhead, and operates from 5:00 a.m. to 30 minutes after sunset. It also takes 50 minutes to complete the entire loop on this route. The Hermits Rest shuttle bus stops at the overlooks and trailheads along Hermit Road on an 80-minute loop. It operates from 5:00 a.m. to 30 minutes after sunset. Shuttle buses run every 15 minutes during peak times, and every half-hour the rest of the day. A shuttle bus map is included in the park newspaper, which is available at the visitor center, and the park entrance stations.

Driving Permits

Two roads along the South Rim also have driving restrictions on them. Hermit Road is closed to private vehicles during the peak season, from March to December. Yaki Point Road and the Kaibab Trailhead parking lot is closed to private vehicles all year. A special access permit is available to visitors with mobility issues, to allow access to these roads. There is no fee for the permit, which is available at the visitor center and the park entrances. The permit must be displayed on the vehicle dashboard when driving on the restricted roads. It does not qualify vehicles to park in accessible parking spaces. A separate placard or license plate is required for that.

Taxi Service

Xanterra Resorts operates a taxi service which serves the Grand Canyon Village, as well as the Tusayan area. Accessible taxis are available upon request, and it's usually only a few minutes wait for one. Advance reservations are not available, but on-call service can be arranged by contacting the Xanterra switchboard at 638-2631, or by stopping by the front desk at any South Rim property.

Wheelchair Rental

Wheelchairs are available for rent at Bright Angel Bicycles, which is located next to the Grand Canyon Visitor Center. Tandem bicycles are also available there. For more information call (928) 814-8704.

Cell Phone Tour

A free cell phone tour of the park can be accessed by calling (928) 225-2907. After you listen to the brief introduction, enter the indicated tour stop number to hear a two-minute interpretative talk by a park ranger. There are 30 stops along the South Rim, Hermit Road, Yaki Point and the North Rim. It should be noted that cell phone service is inconsistent within the park, and although the cell phone tour is free, standard cell charges still apply. It's also worth noting that Verizon is currently the only carrier with access in the park.

Ranger Programs

Free ranger programs are presented daily, and many of them are accessible. The accessible programs are presented at the Yavapai Geology Museum, Mather Point and the Shrine of the Ages, all of which are on a shuttle bus route. See the park newspaper for times and descriptions of the programs.

Attractions

Verkamp's Visitor Center

This 1905 building was once the home to John Verkamp's curio shop, where he hawked souvenirs to Grand Canyon visitors. Today it houses an information desk and a book store, along with some interpretive exhibits that trace the history of the park, from 1870 to the present day. The building features ramp access, with plenty of room to navigate a wheelchair inside. Directional signs also indicate the location of the accessible restrooms.

Hopi House

Built in 1905, Hopi House was the first of eight Mary Colter-designed buildings in the park. The large multi-story building resembles a Hopi pueblo, and it houses a gift shop filled with Native American wares, including a large selection of jewelry, pottery and baskets. The north (canyon side) entrance is accessible, and there is barrier-free access to most of the first-floor areas. One section of the first floor has a few steps down, with no ramp access, and the second floor can only be accessed by a stairway.

Hopi House in Grand Canyon Village

Bright Angel History Room

The Bright Angel History Room is located just off the lobby of the Bright Angel Hotel. There is level access to the room through a wide doorway, and plenty of space to maneuver a wheelchair around the exhibits that illustrate the history of the Fred Harvey Company, El Tovar Hotel and Bright Angel Lodge. Exhibits include artifacts from these two Harvey Houses, as well as old photos, an 1880 Harvey House dinner gong, and even a vintage Harvey Girl uniform. It also includes information and photos about a Harvey Indian Detour excursion, which took train passengers on a five-night trip to nearby Native American sites. The accessible entrance to Bright Angel Lodge is located on the canyon side, as there are stairs up to the front door of this historic building.

Lookout Studio

Lookout Studio was designed in 1914 by Mary Colter, as a gift shop and lookout point for guests of the Fred Harvey Company. There is level access and a wide doorway to the first floor of this rubblestone building, which is precariously perched on the canyon rim. Inside

Fred Harvey Company memorabilia in the Bright Angel History Room

you'll find a small gift shop, and limited views of the canyon. The best views of the canyon are from the front terrace, which can only be accessed by a stairway.

Market Plaza

Market Plaza is located between the Shrine of the Ages and the Grand Canyon Visitor Center. It includes the Yavapai Lodge reception desk and the Canyon Cafe on one side, and the post office, an ATM and the Canyon Village Market on the opposite side. There is level access to all facilities, including the picnic tables near the market. The market has a deli that offers made-to-order sandwiches. It also has a large selection of groceries, beer and wine, camping supplies and souvenirs.

Shrine of the Ages

This multipurpose building is used for meetings, special events, ranger programs and non-denominational church services. There is level access to the entrance, with barrier-free access inside. Both eastbound and westbound shuttle buses stop there.

Entrance to Lookout Studio in Grand Canyon Village

Trails

· ·

Rim Trail
Verkamp's Visitor Center to Lookout Studio

This half-mile stretch of the Rim Trail is paved and level and offers canyon views along the way. It's very crowded, and probably the most popular trail in the park. It passes in front of Hopi House, the El Tovar Hotel, Kachina Lodge, Thunderbird Lodge, the Arizona Room and Bright Angel Lodge. You can do as little or as much of the trail as you like, as it's more of a sidewalk in front of the rim hotels and attractions. Once you hit Lookout Studio, the trail loses its access, so you'll have to double back.

Trail of Time
Yavapai Geology Museum to Verkamp's Visitor Center

The 1.3-mile Trail of Time runs along the existing Rim Trail from the Yavapai Geology Museum to Verkamp's Visitor Center; however access upgrades have been added to make the trail accessible to everyone. The paved level trail winds along the rim of the can-

Accessible scope on the Trail of Time

yon and helps visitors understand the magnitude of geologic time. The geologic timeline is marked by brass medallions embedded in the pavement; and interpretive exhibits and displays along the way encourage visitors to connect the visible rocks in the canyon to the geologic timeline. Wheelchair-height viewing scopes are available, and accessible pictograms point out the wheelchair-accessible route.

Eastern Greenway Trail
South Kaibab Trailhead to Grand Canyon Village

This 4.6-mile section of the Greenway Trail is paved and is open to hikers and cyclists. It's important to note that the shuttle bus drops passengers off at the inaccessible South Kaibib Trailhead. The Eastern Greenway Trail trailhead is located across the street from the shuttle bus stop, near the road and away from the canyon. The paved trail features some undulations and has a 1:8 grade with level spots along the length of it. The slight elevation changes make it interesting, however it's not level like many parts of the Rim Trail.

From the South Kaibib Trailhead it's just a mile to Pipe Creek Vista, with lots of canyon views along the way. There are also benches to sit and rest and enjoy the view at many overlooks. From Pipe Creek

The Eastern Greenway Trail

Vista it's another 1.3 miles to the Grand Canyon Visitor Center. The trail also connects to the Rim Trail at the .9 mile point, and travels another half-mile out to Mather Point. This route is appealing to hikers who want a canyon view, and want to ditch the cyclists (who are not allowed on the Rim Trail). From the Grand Canyon Visitor Center, the Greenway Trail travels through the forest and along the roadside. It's another .8 mile to Market Plaza, an additional .8 mile to Village East, and another .7 mile to Grand Canyon Village. It's also an excellent option for handcyclists.

Western Greenway Trail
Monument Creek to Hermits Rest

The Western Greenway Trail runs from Monument Creek Vista to Hermits Rest, along the canyon on Hermit Road. This 2.8-mile trail is paved, with an accessible grade. The 1.7-mile section from Monument Creek to Pima Point winds through a pinion and juniper woodland and features accessible overlooks along the way. The 1.1-mile stretch from Pima Point to Hermits Rest connects to the paved Rim Trail (where bicycles are prohibited) at the .7 mile point. From there, cyclists are directed to the bicycle lane that runs along Hermit Road.

View from the Western Greenway Trail

Hermit Road Overlooks

The Hermits Rest shuttle bus runs along Hermit Road and stops at nine scenic overlooks along the way. This is a popular route in the afternoon, so for a more relaxed experience, get an early morning start. The shuttle bus stops at all the overlooks on the westbound route, but only at Pima Point, Mohave Point and Powell Point on the eastbound route. Pack along plenty of water, as water bottles can only be refilled at Hermits Rest. The only restrooms along the route are located at Hopi Point and Hermits Rest, so plan accordingly. Hikers can also get off at Monument Creek Vista, and take the accessible Greenway Trail to Hermits Rest.

Trailview Overlook

Located just .7 mile from the Village Route Transfer shuttle bus stop, Trailview Overlook features good views of Grand Canyon Village and the Bright Angel Trail. There are steps down to the lower overlook, but the view is still good from the upper area. If you look real hard, you may be able to see hikers and mules moving along the Bright Angel Trail below.

View from the Powell Point on Hermit Road

Maricopa Point

A wide level asphalt trails leads 150 yards, from the shuttle bus stop out to the overlook, where you can view the Orphan Mine site. This mine first operated as a copper mine from 1891 to 1936; then when a high-grade uranium deposit was discovered in 1951, a private mining company purchased the claim. The uranium mine ceased operation in 1969, and the claim reverted back to the federal government in 1987.

Powell Point

There is a paved level trail out to the overlook at Powell Point, with benches to sit and enjoy the canyon view at the end. There is also a monument dedicated to Major John Wesley Powell, who led the first documented expedition through the Grand Canyon in 1869. The monument has steps up to the top; however the view is just as good from the overlook in front of the monument.

The Abyss on Hermit Road

Hopi Point

Hopi Point is the highest point along Hermit Road. It's also a very popular stop for motorcoaches, so it can get pretty crowded. Accessible restrooms are located in the parking lot, and there is ramp access out to the overlook from the left side of the parking lot. The overlook offers a good view of the Colorado River, but the noise from the motorcoaches and the passengers tends to detract from it a bit.

The Abyss

The Abyss is aptly name, as it features a 3,000 foot sheer drop into the canyon. There is a good view of the canyon and the Colorado River, from the shuttle bus stop all the way out to the viewpoint; however, you have to walk over some rough rock and gravel to get all the way out to the end of the overlook.

Monument Creek Vista

Although there is a step down to the overlook, you can get a good view of Monument Creek from the shuttle bus stop. This is also the starting

View from Hopi Point

point for the 1.7-mile accessible Greenway Trail to Pima Point.

Pima Point

There is level access from the shuttle bus stop to the overlook, which features a good view of Monument Creek Canyon and a piece of the Colorado River. The path that is furthest from the bus stop also leads out to the overlook, however it has a step down. From Pima Point, the accessible Greenway Trail continues for another 1.1 miles to Hermits Rest.

Hermits Rest

Hermits Rest, which was designed by Mary Colter as a rest stop for canyon tourists, is the last stop along Hermit Road. There is level access from the shuttle bus stop down to Hermits Rest, however there are steps leading up into this 1914 building. Inside there is a gift shop and a snack bar, however this National Register of Historic Places building is not wheelchair-accessible. Accessible restrooms are located near the shuttle bus stop. There is also level access to the iconic Hermits Rest Arch, which is located half-way between the restrooms and the shuttle bus stop.

Hermits Rest

Kaibab Rim Route Shuttle Stops

The Kaibab Rim Route shuttle bus runs east and west from the Grand Canyon Visitor Center. Going east it travels along Desert View Drive, and stops at the South Kaibib Trailhead, Yaki Point and Pipe Creek Vista (in that order), before returning to the visitor center. The westbound route includes stops at Mather Point and the Yavapai Geology Museum.

Grand Canyon Visitor Center

There is accessible parking at the Grand Canyon Visitor Center, and level access from the parking area and shuttle bus stop to the entrance. Accessible restrooms are located next to the shuttle bus stop. There is barrier-free access inside the visitor center, which offers interpretive exhibits, a ranger information desk, and a park store. There is also level access to the 20-minute movie, *Grand Canyon: A Journey of Wonder*, which is shown on the hour and half-hour. Accessible seating and companion seats are available in the theater.

Mather Point

Mather Point

Mather Point is one of the best places for sunrise views of the canyon; but to be honest, the views of the Colorado River and the South Kaibib Trail below are great throughout the day. There is a level pathway out to the overlook, and although the trail from the visitor center to the overlook has a slight incline, it's still accessible. Slow walkers who want to skip the walk can take the shuttle.

Yavapai Geology Museum

Perched on the canyon rim, the Yavapai Geology Museum features level access with plenty of room to maneuver a wheelchair inside. The building was constructed in the 1920s, when a group of geologists chose this site as the best representation of Grand Canyon geology. Today the structure houses exhibits about the geology of the area, and offers a great canyon view. Accessible restrooms are located near the parking lot (just follow the sign), and there are also benches to sit down and rest inside the museum.

Yavapai Geology Museum

South Kaibab Trailhead

This is the starting point of the South Kaibib Trail, as well as the accessible Greenway Trail to Pipe Creek Vista. There are some canyon views just down the road from the shuttle bus stop, and although you have to trek out on the dirt to see them, it's doable for most people. Truthfully you'll get much better views along the 1.1-mile trail to Pipe Creek though. Even if you don't want to do the whole trail, at least go around the corner to the first overlook, for a great canyon view.

Yaki Point

Yaki Point offers some nice windshield views of the canyon, and it's a popular alternative to Mather Point for sunrise views. Best bet is to get an accessible driving permit and drive down for sunrise, to avoid the crowds on the early morning shuttle bus.

Pipe Creek Vista

There is a level sidewalk along Pipe Creek Vista, which offers panoramic views of the canyon. From there, you can either take the shuttle bus, or continue along on the Greenway Trail for 1.3 miles to the visitor center.

Lodging

· ·

Accessible Lodging Tips from the Front Desk

Although detailed descriptions of accessible room types are included below, sometimes access is a bit more complicated than just finding a room with a roll-in shower. This is especially true for slow walkers, who may only need a ground floor room. And although special arrangements aren't usually needed for those rooms, the unique architectural features of the South Rim properties make it necessary for slow walkers to reserve ground floor rooms through Central Reservations. With that in mind, I sat down with the front desk supervisor at El Tovar Hotel, and gleaned these insider tips for finding an accessible room that suits your specific access needs.

- Accessible parking is available at all South Rim properties, but it may be difficult to find. The best plan of action is to park in the loading zone in front of the property for registration. From there, front desk personnel will provide a map, with directions to the closest accessible parking areas.

- All of the South Rim properties have bellmen — use them.

- Peak season runs from President's Day to the beginning of November, so plan ahead.

- Portable shower chairs are also available in standard rooms, so make sure and request one when you make your reservation.

- Although many rooms have refrigerators, they are also available in all rooms for medicine storage, upon advance request.

- All accessible rooms are located on the first floor, so a request for an upper floor accessible room cannot be honored.

- Kachina Lodge is the only property with an elevator, so it's a good choice for slow walkers who want an upper floor standard room, but cannot do stairs.

- El Tovar Hotel has a limited number of standard rooms on the ground floor, however they all have a step up into the bathrooms.

- Kachina Lodge and Thunderbird Lodge have steps along the first-floor corridors, so slow walkers should contact Central Reservations to reserve a standard first-floor room on an accessible route.

- Yavapai East and Thunderbird Lodge are the most accessible properties.

- There are no accessible rooms at Bright Angel Lodge or Yavapai West; however all of the rooms at Yavapai West are on one level.

- All of the South Rim properties are air conditioned, except Yavapai West, Maswick South and Bright Angel Lodge.

- Accessible taxis are available to park guests for a nominal fee. Just call the front desk to book one.

- Accessible rooms can only be reserved by phone; however reservation agents are able to interact with property managers to also secure appropriate standard rooms for slow walkers.

- Accessible rooms should be reserved three-to-four months in advance; however if you want an accessible room with a canyon view, you should reserve it as soon as the reservation period opens up, which is 13 months in advance.

- Last but not least, make sure and disclose all of your access needs to Central Reservations. They have a wide variety of accessible rooms, and they will work to find the one that best suits your needs — but they have to know what those needs are.

South Rim Properties

There are six properties on the South Rim, five of which have accessible rooms. El Tovar Hotel, Kachina Lodge and Thunderbird Lodge are located directly on the rim, while Maswick Lodge is about a quarter-mile away. Yavapai Lodge is located near Market Plaza, which is just a short shuttle bus ride from the rim. The properties range from historic to contemporary, and the accessible rooms feature roll-in showers or tub/shower combinations. Not only does each property have its own distinct personality, but the access features at each property are also unique.

El Tovar Hotel

The El Tovar Hotel dates back to 1905, making it the oldest property in the park. It's considered the premier lodging facility at the Grand Canyon, and it has hosted Theodore Roosevelt, Albert Einstein and Zane Grey. This National Historic Landmark has been renovated many times over the years, and today it has wheelchair-accessible rooms with tub/shower combinations.

Room 6439 at the El Tovar Hotel

Bathroom in room 6439 at the El Tovar Hotel

Room 6441 at the El Tovar Hotel

Bathroom in room 6441 at the El Tovar Hotel

The main entrance (which faces Hopi House) has steps, but a ramped accessible entrance is located on the canyon side. Just head towards the flagpole, and turn left when you get to the end of the building.

Room 6439 has wide doorways and good pathway access, and is furnished with a 27-inch high king-sized bed. There is an accessible pathway to the bathroom, which is equipped with a tub/shower combination, with grab bars and a hand-held showerhead, a pedestal sink, and a toilet with grab bars on the left and back walls (as seated). A portable shower bench is also included.

Room 6441 is a deluxe room and is a little larger. It is furnished with two 28-inch high queen-sized beds with pathway access between them. The bathroom configuration is the same as in room 6439, except that the toilet grab bars are located on the back and right walls (as seated). Both rooms also have refrigerators.

Kachina Lodge

Kachina Lodge is located next door to the El Tovar Hotel on the canyon rim. This contemporary property was built in the 1960s, and the

Room 6318 at the Kachina Lodge

Bathroom in room 6318 at the Kachina Lodge

brick interior walls reflect the style of the era. It features wheelchair-accessible rooms with tub/shower combinations.

There's no front desk for this property, so guests check-in at the El Tovar Hotel. Room 6318 features a 26-inch high king-sized bed, with good pathway access throughout the room. It has a wide front door, a sliding door to the bathroom, and a refrigerator. The bathroom has a tub/shower combination with a hand-held showerhead, grab bars and a portable shower chair. The toilet grab bars are located on the back and right walls (as seated). Other access features include a roll-under sink and a lowered mirror.

As noted earlier, the Kachina Lodge is also the only property in the park with an elevator, so it's a good choice for slow walkers who want a standard room on an upper floor.

Thunderbird Lodge

Located next door to Kachina Lodge, The Thunderbird Lodge is identical in style and ambiance. This property has wheelchair-accessible rooms with roll-in showers or tub/shower combinations. It is also the only property in the park that has wheelchair-accessible rooms with canyon views.

Room 6213 at the Thunderbird Lodge

Bathroom in room 6213 at the Thunderbird Lodge

Like the Kachina Lodge, there's no front desk at the Thunderbird Lodge, so guests check-in at the Bright Angel Lodge. Although the main entrance to the Bright Angel Lodge has steps, the canyon side entrance is barrier-free.

Room 6213 has wide doorways and good pathway access. It is furnished with two 26-inch high queen-sized beds, with good pathway access between them. There is a sliding door to the bathroom, which is equipped with a roll-in shower with a hand-held showerhead, grab bars and a portable shower chair. The toilet grab bars are located on the back and right walls (as seated), and the bathroom also has a roll-under sink.

Room 6211 has the same access features, except that it also has a second door which opens out to the canyon.

Room 6209 has the same access features as room 6213, except that the bathroom is equipped with a tub/shower combination.

The rooms also all have refrigerators.

Additionally, all of the accessible rooms in the Thunderbird Lodge have electronic draperies. These can be operated from a lowered switch located next to the thermostat, or with a slight tug to the drapery.

Maswick Lodge

Maswick Lodge is more of a motel-style property, with parking located right outside the rooms. The property is spread out between buildings dotted throughout a pine forest. It is divided into north and south sections, with the north section being the newer of the two. The north section has wheelchair-accessible rooms with roll-in showers or tub/shower combinations, while the south section has wheelchair-accessible rooms with tub/shower combinations. There is level access to the main lobby, with accessible parking located nearby.

The north section houses Room 6761 in the Cliffrose building, which is located near the main lobby. There is accessible parking in front, with level access to the room. It is furnished with two 22-inch queen-sized beds, with good pathway access between them. It also has a sliding glass door, with level access out to a small patio area. The room also includes a refrigerator.

Room 6761 at the Maswick Lodge

Bathroom in room 6761 at the Maswick Lodge

The bathroom has a roll-in shower with grab bars, a hand-held showerhead and a fold-down shower bench. The toilet grab bars are located on the back and left walls (as seated). Other access features include a roll-under sink and a lowered mirror and hair dryer.

Room 6892 in the Spruce building is also located in the north section. There is level access to the room from a nearby accessible parking space. It is furnished with two 22-inch high queen-sized beds, with an access aisle between them. It also has level access to the small patio through the sliding glass door, and a refrigerator.

The bathroom is equipped with a tub/shower combination, with grab bars and a portable shower chair. It also includes a toilet with grab bars on the back and left walls (as seated), a roll-under sink and a lowered mirror.

The south section houses room 6610, located in building 1, which is also close to the main lobby. There is level access to the room from the nearby accessible parking space.

Room 6892 at the Maswick Lodge

Bathroom in room 6892 at the Maswick Lodge

Room 6610 at the Maswick Lodge

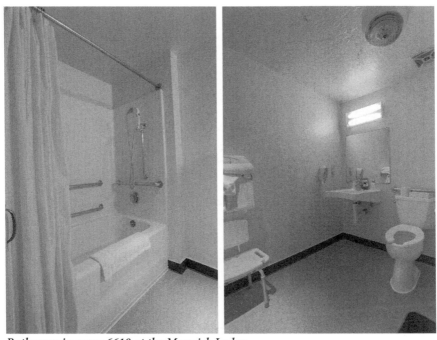

Bathroom in room 6610 at the Maswick Lodge

33

It's furnished with two queen-sized beds with an access aisle between them, and a refrigerator. There is good pathway access throughout the room, with a sliding door into the bathroom. The bathroom has a tub/shower combination with a hand-held showerhead, grab bars and a portable shower chair. The toilet grab bars are located on the back and left walls (as seated). It also includes a roll-under sink and a lowered mirror.

Yavapai Lodge

Yavapai Lodge is divided into east and west sections, with the east section having wheelchair-accessible rooms with roll-in showers or tub/shower combinations. It's located in a small pine forest, and a bit off-the-beaten-path, but it's still accessible by the free park shuttle. The registration desk is located in Market Plaza, which is a short drive away from the rooms. There is accessible parking in front, with level access up to the main lobby.

There is accessible parking in the Yavapai East section, with level access to the rooms. Room 7370, which is located in building 4, features wide doorways and good pathway access. It's equipped with a refrig-

Room 7370 at the Yavapai Lodge

Bathroom in room 7370 at the Yavapai Lodge

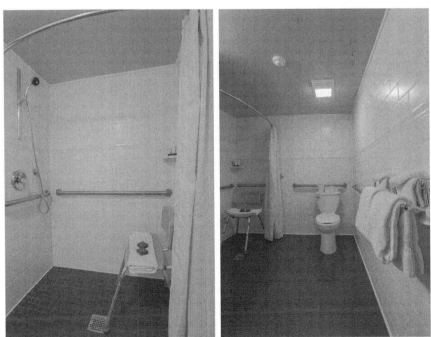

Bathroom in room 7420 at the Yavapai Lodge

erator and furnished with two 26-inch high queen-sized beds, with an access aisle between them. Other access features include drapery wands, and an automatic door opener.

There is level access to the bathroom through a wide sliding door. The bathroom is equipped with a tub/shower combination with a hand-held showerhead, grab bars and a portable shower bench. The toilet grab bars are located on the left and back walls (as seated), and the bathroom also includes a roll-under sink.

Room 7420, which is located in building 5, includes the same access features as room 7370, except that it has a roll-in shower.

Dining

El Tovar Dining Room

There is ramp access to the El Tovar Dining Room from the lobby, with plenty of room to navigate a wheelchair in the spacious and elegant restaurant. They serve breakfast, lunch and dinner, and it's the only Grand Canyon restaurant that accepts dinner reservations (928-638-2631). The menu is traditional, yet it has a definite Southwestern flair, with items such as Salmon Tostadas, Navajo Tacos and Sonoran Style Eggs with Chorizo. Breakfast is a real treat in this fine dining establishment, with perfectly cooked-to-order eggs, and the most experienced servers in the park.

Arizona Room

Located on the canyon rim between the Bright Angel Lodge and Thunderbird Lodge, the Arizona Room serves lunch and dinner. The main entrance has steps down into the restaurant, but there is a level accessible entrance on the canyon side. The menu features soups, salads, sandwiches and select entrees at lunch; and everything from Adobo Chicken to Filet Mignon at dinner. Although the dinner menu is more extensive, lunch can be a real treat with the panoramic canyon view.

Bright Angel Restaurant

This casual coffee shop is located in the Bright Angel Lodge, with ramp access up from the lobby area. It's open year-round for breakfast, lunch and dinner. This is a good choice if you are watching your calories, as select menu items contain nutritional information. Burgers, fajitas and sandwiches are the mainstay of this family-style restaurant, but they also offer chicken, pasta, beef and Southwestern entrees. It's a good place for a quick bite, and an excellent choice for parents with kids in tow.

Maswick Food Court

The Maswick Food Court features several stations that offer plated lunches and dinners, salads and sandwiches to go, cooked-to-order breakfast dishes, and light snacks. There is level access to the food court from the front lobby, with ample room to navigate a wheelchair in the serving and seating areas. Healthy options are available at most stations, including fruit, oatmeal, cereal, gluten-free buns and veggie burgers. Next door there is level access to the Pizza Pub which serves up pizza, salad, beer and wine until 11:00 p.m. The Pizza Pub keeps the latest hours in the park, so it's a good choice for late arrivals.

Canyon Cafe

Located at the Yavapai Lodge, the Canyon Cafe features ramp access from the front lobby, and level access from the parking area. It is open seasonally for breakfast, lunch and dinner. Selections include soups, sandwiches and entrees, such as baked chicken, pot pies and hamburgers. On the healthy side, a self-serve salad bar is also available. And if you'd like to enjoy lunch along the trail, they also offer box lunches to go.

Tours

Xanterra Bus Tours

If you'd rather leave the driving to someone else, Xanterra offers a number of narrated bus tours that depart from Grand Canyon Village. Accessible buses are available with 48-hours advance notice, but it's best to reserve space as far in advance as possible, as these popular tours fill up quickly.

The one-and-a-half-hour Sunset Tour offers a good introduction to the South Rim, as it includes an overview of the village area and the historic architecture of Mary Colter. It also touches on the human history of the Grand Canyon. The highlight of the tour is the sunset at Yaki Point or Mohave Point, two of the most panoramic South Rim viewpoints.

The two-hour Hermits Rest Tour travels along this old wagon road built by the Santa Fe Railway. The tour stops at Hermits Rest, as well as several other viewpoints along the way.

Accessible Xanterra tour bus

The Desert View Tour takes nearly four hours, as it covers the entire length of Desert View Drive. The tour stops at Lipan Point, for a spectacular view of the Colorado River, as well as Desert View, the location of the historic Watchtower.

The one-and-a-half-hour Sunrise Tour covers the west end of the park, and focuses on the geology of the canyon. While waiting for the sunrise, the guide answers questions, and points out the best vantage points for sunrise photos.

Helicopter and Airplane Tours

If you'd like to get a bird's eye view of the canyon, Papillon Grand Canyon Helicopters has a few tours that might work for some wheelchair-users and slow walkers. All of the South Rim air tours depart from the Grand Canyon National Park Airport, which is located in Tusayan, just outside of the park.

There is level access to the Papillon office at the heliport, with barrier-free access out to the helicopters and airplanes.

Helicopter landing at Papillon Grand Canyon Helicopters

The South Rim Airplane Tour is the most accessible option, and this 50 minute tour includes views of the Zuni Corridor, Imperial Point, the Confluence of the Colorado and Little Colorado Rivers, Kaibab National Forest and Kaibab Plateau. It is conducted in a Vistaliner aircraft, with large windows, so there's not a bad seat in the house. There are six stairs up to the aircraft door, but a lift is available for anyone who can't manage the climb. Most power and manual wheelchairs can be carried in the cargo hold, on a space-available basis. And as with all of the Papillon tours, disabled passengers must be accompanied by an able-bodied attendant.

Lift boarding is not available on the helicopter tours. If a passenger is unable to board on his own, his attendant must be able to assist, as the crew is prohibited from lifting passengers. Manual wheelchairs with removable wheels can be carried on most flights, but power wheelchairs cannot be accommodated. All wheelchairs are carried on a space-available basis.

The North Canyon Helicopter Tour features a loop route over the Colorado River to the North Rim. This 25-minute tour includes views of the Tower of Ra, Vishnu Schist, and Dragon Corridor, the widest and deepest section of the Grand Canyon.

The Imperial Helicopter Tour lasts for 45 minutes, and includes sweeping views of the canyon and Kaibab National Forest. The route takes guests by Point Imperial, over the North Rim, and then back through the canyon's central regions.

Both tours can also be done on the larger Eco Star EC 130 helicopter. These helicopters feature forward facing stadium seats with almost an 180 degree view. It's the first-class way to see the Grand Canyon.

Resources

General Information

(928) 638-7888
www.nps.gov/grca

Road Conditions

(928) 638-7496

Central Reservations (lodging and bus tours)

Xanterra Parks & Resorts
(888) 297-2757
www.grandcanyonlodges.com

Papillon Helicopter Tours

(888) 635-7272
www.papillon.com

Desert View Drive

Although Desert View Drive is technically part of the South Rim, it can also be accessed from the east park entrance, located 30 miles west of Cameron, Arizona. Named after the historic Desert View Watchtower, the road runs from the South Entrance Road in the west, to the east park gate. Along the way you'll be treated to sweeping views of the Colorado River, some native American ruins and an interesting museum. Unlike the South Rim proper, there's no shuttle bus service to this section of the park, however many of the viewpoints and attractions are accessible. Additionally, you'll find many stunning windshield views along the way. It's a good choice for people who want to ditch the crowds for a day, or for folks who want to exit through the east gate and continue along over the Hopi reservation to Southern Colorado.

Attractions

Desert View Visitor Center

Located at the eastern end of Desert View Drive, the Desert View Visitor Center features interpretive exhibits, an information desk and a large bookstore and gift shop. It's a good place to get oriented if you are entering the park from the east entrance, but it's worth a stop even if you've already stopped by the Grand Canyon Visitor Center on the South Rim. There is plenty of accessible parking in the large lot in front of the visitor center, with a level pathway to the entrance. Both the front and back entrances are accessible, so you can stop in on your way to or from the Desert View Watchtower.

Desert View Watchtower

The iconic Desert View Watchtower is located about a quarter-mile from the Desert View Visitor Center, down a paved trail. That said, the trail has a sustained 1:8 grade, with no level spots along the way. It's quite doable for power wheelchair- and scooter-users, however, manual wheelchair-users may need a bit of assistance on the trek back up to the parking lot. There is level access to the Trading Post, which is located midway along the trail. Accessible restrooms are

Desert View Watchtower

located near the Trading Post, however there is a shorter accessible route to them from the passenger drop-off area. There is level access to the first floor of the Desert View Watchtower; however the upper floors are only accessible by stairs. There is a small gift shop inside the watchtower, which was originally designed as a rest area by Mary Colter in 1932. Colter envisioned the structure as something that would blend in with the surrounding landscape, so the view of the watchtower is just as impressive, as the view from inside it. There is also level access to the overlook in front of the watchtower, which affords some magnificent views of the Grand Canyon.

Tusayan Museum

The Tusayan Museum and pueblo site is located between Lipan Point and Moran Point, on the south side of the road. There are two accessible parking areas; one near the accessible family restroom, and the other near the entrance to the museum. There is level access from both parking areas to the museum, which features exhibits about the ancestral pueblo people who inhabited the site 800 years ago. Although there is plenty of room to navigate a wheelchair through

Tusayan Museum

the museum, it can get a little crowded during peak season. Outside, a short paved accessible trail winds around the former pueblo site, with interpretive signs along the way.

Overlooks

Navajo Point

Navajo Point, which is located just west of Desert View, is probably the least accessible overlook along the road. There is no accessible parking there; in fact, there is no striping at all in the parking lot. The curbs are approximately eight-inches high, with no curb-cut access to the overlook. There is a semi-accessible path out to the overlook on one side, however it's bumpy with a few steps here and there. It may be doable for someone who uses a cane, with some assistance; but wheelchair-users would be hard-pressed to make it out to the overlook. This is the highest overlook along Desert View Drive at 7,461 feet, and it offers a good view of the nearby Desert View Watchtower, as well as the canyon below.

Moran Point overlook

Lipan Point

Lipan Point, which is located west of Navajo Point, has slightly better access; however, it's still not technically wheelchair-accessible. There is no accessible parking, although at least this lot is striped. Like Navajo Point, there are no curb-cuts, and you have to be able to navigate an eight-inch curb to access the overlook. The path out to the overlook is uneven and bumpy, and there are a couple of steps along the way. The upside of this overlook is that if you pull into one or two prime parking spaces you will get a good windshield view of the Colorado River in the canyon below; however, the overlook itself is not accessible for most wheelchair-users.

Moran Point

Moving west on Desert View Drive, the next overlook is Moran Point. There is accessible parking, with curb-cut access up to an asphalt path which leads out to the overlook. The path on the right side of the parking lot is the accessible one, as the one on the left has a few steps along the way. The overlook offers a nice view of the Colorado River, and you can even spot Cape Royal on the North Rim, eight

Grandview Point overlook

miles across the canyon. This overlook also offers a good example of the layered Paleozoic sedimentary rock that makes up the lion's share of the Grand Canyon.

BuggeIn

BuggeIn is a picnic area that is located west of Moran Point. There is accessible parking located near the accessible restroom, however there is absolutely no canyon view at this rest stop. There is an accessible picnic table there, but it's located in a dirt area at the end of a bumpy path with a slight incline. It's a good stop if you need to use the restroom, but that's about it.

Grandview Point

Grandview Point is the most popular stop along Desert View Drive, but it's also one of the more accessible overlooks. There's accessible parking, with curb-cut access to the paved path which leads out to the overlook. Along the way there are interpretive panels about the Last Chance Copper Claim, which was located 3,000 feet below the rim and operated from 1890 to 1907, and the Grand View Hotel which graced this site in the late 1800s. Grandview Point also offers sweeping panoramic views of the Grand Canyon, including several bends in the Colorado River. Accessible restrooms are also located near the accessible parking spots.

Desert View Drive Picnic Area

Although this picnic area is the most accessible one along Desert View Drive, it doesn't have an official name. It is however depicted on the park map with a picnic table pictogram. It's located near milepost 234, close to the intersection of Yaki Point Road. It's surrounded by trees, and includes accessible parking, an accessible restroom and an accessible picnic table. There is level access out to the picnic table and to the restroom. The down side to this picnic area is that it's also a popular parking place for hikers who venture out to Yaki Point. Still, it's a beautiful place for a picnic, if you can find a parking spot.

Grand Canyon Railway

If you'd like to leave the driving to someone else, then head up to the South Rim on the Grand Canyon Railway. This historic excursion runs along Highway 64, and travels from Williams to Grand Canyon Village. Although the railway dates back to 1901, access upgrades have been added over the years, so today it's a suitable option for wheelchair-users and slow walkers. And with a variety of packages available, you can opt to spend the afternoon in the park, or extend your stay and overnight in one of the accessible South Rim properties.

The Route

The Grand Canyon Railway departs from the historic Williams Depot, located right behind the Grand Canyon Railway Hotel. Although there is an accessible pathway from the hotel to the depot, cart transportation is available if you can't manage the distance. Arrangements for cart transportation should be made in advance though, as things can get hectic near departure time.

The Cataract Creek Gang engaging in a shoot-out before the departure of the Grand Canyon Railway

A portable lift provides access to all classes of cars

There is level access to the train depot, gift shop and coffee stand, and an accessible restroom is located in the back. Prior to the morning departure from the Williams Depot, there is a wild west shootout, which features the local marshal and the nefarious Cataract Creek Gang. There is level access to the show area, which is located next to the depot. Wheelchair-accessible seating is available for the show, in front of the bleachers or at nearby tables.

After the show, a preboarding announcement is made, and wheelchair-users and slow walkers are boarded before the rest of the passengers. On the trip up, passengers in first class, the observation dome and the parlor car are served a continental breakfast; and on the way back they are treated to appetizers and champagne. A cash bar is also available. Soft drinks are served on both legs in the Budd and Pullman cars.

During the two-hour journey, roving musicians entertain passengers with western songs, and on-board attendants are available to field questions about activities at the South Rim. And on the return trip, the Cataract Creek Gang makes an encore appearance, as they attempt to rob the train.

Parlor car on the Grand Canyon Railway

The train makes two daily round-trips to the South Rim in the summer; and one a day the rest of the year. Most people go up and back on the same day, but you can also purchase a package that includes overnight accommodations in an accessible room at Maswick Lodge. Alternatively, you can also extend your South Rim stay for several days if you like, as trains run up and back every day.

Access Aboard

Access is good on this historic train; and train buffs are wowed by the vintage train cars, which are pulled by a steam engine during the summer, and a diesel locomotive the rest of the year. There are five classes of service, with coach and first class being the most accessible.

The Pullman coach cars have bench seats and windows that open, while the Budd coach cars have bench seats and air conditioning. The first-class cars have comfortable reclining seats, large windows and air conditioning. All three types of cars can be accessed by a portable lift, and they all have wheelchair tie-downs, nearby companion seats and a restroom with grab bars, a wide doorway and ample room to transfer. Power outlets are located near the accessible seats, and the lifts are large enough to accommodate scooters and heavy power wheelchairs.

The parlor car and the observation dome are also accessible by the portable lift; however both are more appropriate for slow walkers. The parlor car has table-and-chair seating, with no tie-downs, so a transfer is necessary; while the observation dome has seven steps to the top. And of course, if you just can't make up your mind, you can always mix classes; and take one class going up and another on the return trip.

Accessible toilet aboard the Grand Canyon Railway

The reservation and on-board staff is very accommodating, so make sure and let them know if you have any access needs; especially if you are a slow walker or your disability isn't apparent. They are also happy to answer questions and even provide suggestions to help make your trip more comfortable.

Grand Canyon Railway Hotel

Because of its close proximity to the depot, the Grand Canyon Railway hotel is an excellent lodging choice for a pre- or post-excursion stay. The 297-room hotel features excellent access, and it's just a block away from downtown Williams and historic Route 66. There is accessible parking near the entrance, with level access to the lobby. Accessible accommodations are available in standard rooms or suites.

Standard Rooms

The accessible standard rooms are very roomy at 327 square feet, and they feature wide doorways, good pathway access, lowered closet rods, lever handles and a lowered peephole. They are furnished with 24-inch high beds, with wheelchair access around them.

The bathrooms include a full five-foot turning radius, and are equipped with a roll-in shower or a tub/shower combination. Other access features include a hand-held showerhead, grab bars in the shower and around the toilet, a portable shower bench and a roll-under sink.

Suites

Suite 1326, which is located on the ground floor, is the most accessible suite. It features wide doorways, a lowered peephole and good pathway access to all areas of the room. It's equipped with a kitchenette with a refrigerator, a microwave and a wet bar; and a sitting area with a sleeper-sofa, coffee table and a flat screen TV. The sofa can sleep two people, and when it's unfolded the bed is 14-inches high.

Living area of suite 1326 at the Grand Canyon Railway hotel

Bedroom in suite 1326 at the Grand Canyon Railway hotel

The spacious guest bedroom features two 27-inch high queen-sized beds, with a wheelchair accessible pathway between them. There's plenty of room to navigate a wheelchair in the room, and it's furnished with a desk with a chair, night tables, an easy chair and an armoire with a flat-screen TV. The environmental controls are wheelchair height, and the draperies feature easy-to-reach wands for opening and closing.

Bathroom in suite 1326 at the Grand Canyon Railway hotel

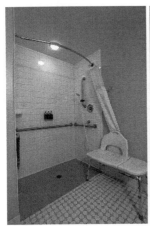

The bathroom is equipped with a roll-in shower with a hand-held showerhead, grab bars and an adjustable shower chair. Other access features include toilet grab bars on the right and back walls (as seated), and a roll-under sink.

Public Areas

Access is good to all the public areas at the Grand Canyon Railway Hotel, including the lobby and outdoor areas. The pool and spa are equipped with lifts, and there's plenty of room to roll around on the level deck.

The Grand Depot Cafe, which is located near the depot, features ramp access, with plenty of room to maneuver inside. This buffet-style restaurant serves breakfast, lunch and dinner, and features a fresh selection of traditional fare, as well as an evening carving station and pasta bar. And if you need help carrying your tray, staff members are happy to assist.

There is also level access to Spenser's Pub, which is located near the lobby in the main hotel building. This casual eatery offers a light bar menu and a large selection of libations. Patio dining is also available during the warmer months.

Customer service is top-drawer at the Grand Canyon Railway Hotel too, so don't be afraid to ask if you need anything. The bottom line is, the Grand Canyon Railway Hotel is a very comfortable, accessible and friendly place to stay; on your way to or from the South Rim.

Resources

Grand Canyon Railway

(800) 843-8726
www.thetrain.com

North Rim

Only 10 percent of the visitors to Grand Canyon National Park venture over to the remote North Rim. Located south of Jacob Lake, it's only a four-hour drive from Las Vegas, however the road to the park is only open from May 15 to October 15. Still, there are several scenic drives, as well as accessible lodging options, in this quieter, more secluded section of the park.

Attractions

Visitor Center

The best place to begin your North Rim visit is at the North Rim Visitor Center, which is located near the end of the road, down the street from the lodge. There is ramp access up to the visitor center, with accessible parking available in the adjacent lot. Inside, you'll find interpretive exhibits, maps, brochures and a bookstore. A ranger is on duty to field questions, and a variety of interpretive programs are held there. A loaner wheelchair is also available on a first-come basis.

Grand Canyon North Rim Visitor Center

Point Imperial Scenic Drive

Since it's not as developed as the South Rim, the main accessible activity on the North Rim is taking a scenic drive. At the top of the list is the Point Imperial Scenic Drive, which runs 11 miles, from the visitor center out to Point Imperial. Point Imperial is the highest point in the park, at 8,803 feet, and it offers spectacular windshield views of Mt. Hayden and Marble Canyon. There is also an accessible restroom there. Take your time along this drive, as the scenery is pleasant along the way.

Cape Royal Scenic Drive

The longer Cape Royal Scenic Drive also starts at the visitor center and travels past the Point Imperial turnoff, out to Cape Royal. It's 32 miles (one-way) and can easily be combined with the Point Imperial scenic drive, for a full-day excursion. This drive offers a panoramic view up, down and across the canyon, with scenic windshield views available at Vista Encantada, Roosevelt Point and Walhalla Overlook. There is an accessible viewpoint and restroom at Cape Royal that can be accessed by a paved level trail. The Desert View Watchtower can be easily spotted across the canyon, from this viewpoint. This drive has a lot of curves, and the maximum vehicle length is 30 feet. It may also be closed in inclement weather, especially when there are high winds.

Lodging

Located along the North Rim of the canyon, Grand Canyon Lodge offers several accessible cabins. There's level access to the main lodge, and with an accessible parking placard you can park in front while you check-in.

The most accessible cabins are Western Cabins 356 and 348, which are located closest to the accessible parking area behind the visitor center. They are furnished with a queen-sized bed, a desk and a chair; and also include a fireplace and a refrigerator. And for your lounging comfort, there are two rocking chairs on the private front porch.

Access features include wide doorways, level thresholds and good pathway access. The bathrooms are equipped with a roll-in shower, grab bars and a hand-held showerhead. There is also a roll-under sink. Toilet grab bars are located on the back and right walls (as seated), and a portable shower chair is available upon request.

The other two accessible Western Cabins (315 and 317) are located closer to the lodge and rim, but further from the accessible parking area. They have the same access features as cabins 356 and 348, except that tub/shower combinations with fold-down shower seats replace the roll-in showers.

Two accessible Pioneer Cabins (5 and 38) were also added in 2009. They are equipped with roll-in showers and have the same access features as the Western Cabins. These one-bedroom cabins have plenty of room to maneuver a wheelchair and they are furnished with one double bed and one twin bed.

One Frontier Cabin (84) also has access features, including wide doorways and good pathway access. The bathroom is equipped with a roll-in shower with grab bars and a hand-held showerhead. It also

Cabins at Grand Canyon North Rim

has toilet grab bars and a roll-under sink. A portable shower chair is available upon request.

Another Frontier Cabin (29) may work for some slow walkers. It doesn't have wide doorways, but it does have a low-step (five-inch) shower with a corner shower seat, grab bars and a hand-held shower-head. There's a toilet grab bar on the back wall, with an additional set attached to the toilet seat. A roll-under sink is also included.

These comfortable cabins are surrounded by trees, so you really get the feeling that you are in the great outdoors. You may even spot a deer or two wandering around in the morning.

But by far, one of the best features of this property is its location. Since it's perched on the canyon rim, it offers an excellent view. The wheelchair-accessible sun porch in the main lodge is the perfect place to enjoy it all. It's especially impressive at sunset.

Dining

Grand Canyon Lodge Dining Room

The Grand Canyon Lodge Dining Room serves breakfast, lunch and dinner and features regional cuisine and 1930s-themed foods. There is lift access to the dining room, which is located inside the main lodge. A buffet is also available during breakfast and lunch. The breakfast buffet offers an assortment of hot and cold breakfast items, and the lunch buffet includes a salad bar and an assortment of pastas and sauces. An a la carte menu is also available at all meals.

Roughrider Saloon

The Roughrider Saloon offers light snacks and assorted libations in the afternoon and evening. There is level access to the saloon from the back of the main lodge building. There is also level access from the saloon to a small coffee shop, which offers coffee and pastries in the morning.

Grand Canyon Cookout Experience

And if you want to enjoy a tasty barbeque dinner in the great out-doors, then make sure and sign up for the Grand Canyon Cookout Experience (GCCE). Held nightly from June 1 to September 30, this fun event features a hearty chuck wagon-style dinner and plenty of cowboy entertainment. The all you can eat buffet includes smoked beef brisket, roasted chicken, potatoes, beans, cornbread, salad, macaroni and cheese, vegetables, cole slaw, cucumber salad, vegetar-ian chili, watermelon, cookies, lemonade, ice tea and coffee. Trans-portation to and from the accessible dining tent is provided in the lift-equipped GCCE steam train tram. It's great fun, and I guarantee you won't go away hungry. Advance reservations are required. They can be made at the front desk, or by calling (928) 638-2611.

Resources

General Information

(928) 638-7888
www.nps.gov/grca

Lodging

Forever Resorts
(877) 386-4383
www.grandcanyonlodgenorth.com

Grand Canyon West

Just a three-hour drive from Las Vegas, Grand Canyon West is the newest development in the Grand Canyon area. Located entirely on Hualapai land, it features the infamous skywalk, overnight lodging, food and beverage outlets and lots of spectacular views. Although it's located on tribal land and exempt from the Americans with Disabilities Act, access is surprisingly good there. Unfortunately the last nine miles of the road isn't paved yet, but it is graded and well maintained, so it's suitable for low clearance vehicles. The drive is also quite scenic, as the route passes through a massive Joshua tree forest.

The Basics

Getting There

From Las Vegas, go south on US-93 for 72 miles, then turn left on Pierce Ferry Road. Follow Pierce Ferry Road for 28 miles, then turn right on Diamond Bar Road. From there it's a 21-mile drive to Grand Canyon West. The drive takes between two and three hours.

From Kingman, head north on Stockton Hill Road for 42 miles, and then turn right on Pierce Ferry Road. Follow Pierce Ferry Road for 7 miles, then turn right on Diamond Bar Road. From there it's a 21 mile drive to Grand Canyon West. The drive takes approximately one-and-a-half hours.

Main Terminal

Once you arrive at Grand Canyon West, you will be directed to a parking area outside of the Main Terminal. Private vehicles are not allowed beyond this point, so you'll have to park your car and take the shuttle bus from there. There's plenty of accessible parking near the Main Terminal, with level access from the parking lot. Inside, you'll find a gift shop, a snack bar, accessible restrooms and a ticket counter. The shuttle bus stop is located behind the main terminal, with a level pathway leading from the building.

Prices and Packages

Since Grand Canyon West is located on tribal land, national park passes are not valid there. All visitors must purchase either a Hualapai Legacy or Hualapai Gold admission package to gain entrance to the public areas of the park. The Hualapai Legacy package ($44.05) includes shuttle bus transportation to Eagle Point, Guano Point and Hualapai Ranch, but does not include admission to the skywalk. The Legacy Gold package ($87.81) includes all of the benefits of the Hualapai Legacy package, plus admission to the skywalk, and lunch at the viewpoint of your choice. All of the Grand Canyon West restaurants also accept cash, and no outside food is allowed in the park.

Shuttle Bus

Access to the public areas of the park is only available by the park shuttle. Buses carry visitors from the Main Terminal to Eagle Point, Guano Point and Hualapai Ranch. Accessible kneeling buses with ramp access are available. They are equipped with tie-downs and can accommodate up to four wheelchair-users. The tribe is currently in the process of purchasing more accessible buses, and they hope to

Accessible shuttle transports visitors to the sites of Grand Canyon West

have the entire fleet accessible by the summer of 2014. These hop-on hop-off buses run every 15 minutes, so you can spend as much time at each stop as you want.

Eagle Point

Eagle Point is the first shuttle bus stop, and the first thing you will notice when you arrive is the spectacular canyon view. Named for the eagle rock formation on the canyon wall, Eagle Point is a very sacred place to the Hualapai people. They believe that the spirit of the eagle delivers prayers from people to the heavens. Out of respect, they have kept the canyon rim in pristine condition, so you won't find the requisite sidewalks and guard rails that are prolific on the South Rim. Although the parking area is covered in gravel, it's a level roll from the shuttle bus stop over to the canyon rim. It's a little bumpy, so some people may need assistance, but the view is great from just about every spot along the rim. Additionally, you'll find Hualapai ambassadors dressed in traditional clothing at all the sites. They are there to interact with visitors, answer questions, and share their culture and traditions, so don't be afraid to approach them.

Eagle Point at Grand Canyon West

Grand Canyon Skywalk

The highlight of Eagle Point is the Grand Canyon Skywalk, a u-shaped glass bridge that extends out over the canyon. There is ramp access up to the ticket line, and level access to the adjacent locker area. Nothing is permitted out on the skywalk, so all purses, cameras, backpacks and bags must be left in the lockers. Ambulatory visitors are asked to wear disposable booties on the skywalk, but there are no restrictions for wheelchair-users. From the locker area, you can just roll right out to the skywalk, and get a bird's eye view of the canyon below. It's truly a once-in-a-lifetime experience, and you can take as much time on the skywalk as you want. And since cameras are prohibited on the skywalk, staff photographers are on hand to photograph visitors.

Skywalk Cafe

There is a level pathway from the skywalk over to the Skywalk Cafe, which offers a nice selection of casual lunch fare. Menu choices include a roast beef or turkey sandwich served with fresh fruit, potato chips, trail mix and a medium drink, as well as vegetarian selections

Grand Canyon Skywalk at Eagle Point

Visitors on the Grand Canyon Skywalk at Eagle Point

such as salads, a black bean burger or stir fried vegetables and rice. There is level access to the outside seating area, with accessible restrooms located nearby.

Amphitheater

There is a barrier-free pathway from the skywalk to the amphitheater, where tribal members from across the nation perform traditional songs and dances. The performers are dressed in traditional regalia as they perform favorites such as the Hoop Dance, the Grass Dance and the Hualapai Bird Dance. The amphitheater is partially shaded, so it's also a good place to take a break from the sun.

Native American Village

The Native American Village, which is located near the amphitheater, features a collection of traditional dwellings hand-crafted by tribal members. It includes a Navajo Hogan, a Havasupai Sweat Lodge, a Plains Tipi, a Hopi House, and a Hualapai Wikiup. There is an accessible path through the village, and you can roll right up to the dwellings and even have a look inside.

Guano Point

Guano Point, which is the second shuttle bus stop, is the site of an abandoned bat guano mining venture. In 1958 U.S. Guano Corporation constructed a tramway system to extract the guano from a cave below the rim. Shortly after all the guano was extracted, an Air Force jet collided with the overhead cable system, so all that's left today are the towers. Today, you can get a great view of the canyon from the rim; however the walk out to the very tip of Guano Point is pretty rugged and not wheelchair-accessible.

Guano Point Buffet

There is level access to the Guano Point Buffet, which offers a substantial BBQ beef or baked chicken lunch. It's accompanied with mixed vegetables, salad, mashed potatoes and gravy, a dinner roll, dessert and a beverage. There is level access to the covered outside seating area, and since it's located on the canyon rim, the view is excellent. Accessible restrooms are located nearby.

The Hopi House in the Native American Village at Grand Canyon West

Hualapai Market

There is level access over to the Hualapai Market, which is located next to the Guano Point Buffet. The pathway is dirt and gravel, but it's doable for most people. Inside, there's plenty of room to roll around and browse through the wares of the Native American vendors. The quality is good and the prices are very reasonable, but make sure and bring cash, because they don't accept credit cards.

Hualapai Ranch

Hualapai Ranch is the last shuttle bus stop; however, you can also drive there, because it's located outside the vehicle-free zone. It's about a mile from the Main Terminal, as you approach Grand Canyon West. It's also the site of the closest overnight accommodations.

Western Village

This re-creation of a western village features old time store fronts, horse stables, covered wagons and employees outfitted in western gear. Parking is available just outside the village in a large un-striped

Entrance to Hualapai Ranch

dirt parking area. The shuttle bus stops near a short dirt pathway that leads to the village. There is ramp access up to the boardwalk sidewalks inside the village, and most of the buildings have level access. You can also easily wheel around in the dirt in front of the store fronts, as there isn't any vehicle traffic through the town. Wranglers are on hand to teach visitors the finer points of roping, or show them how to toss a tomahawk. Wagon and horseback rides are also available, but they are not accessible.

Dance Hall & Dining Room

The dining room is located on the far end of town. There is a wide doorway at the entrance, and the one-inch threshold is easy to bump over. Inside, there is plenty of room to maneuver a wheelchair. Lunch and dinner are served in the dining room, accompanied by musical entertainment. Meal choices include BBQ ribs or baked chicken, served with beans, mashed potatoes, mixed vegetables, cornbread, a cookie and a non-alcoholic beverage. Alcohol is not served anywhere at Grand Canyon West; in fact it's prohibited on tribal land.

Western Cabins

Overnight lodging is available in Western Cabins, which are located past the dining room in a remote area of the village. Guests check-in at the telegraph office in the village. There is ramp access up to the boardwalk sidewalk, but there is a small step at the office entrance. The office can also be accessed through the gift shop next door, which has a level entry. There is no parking in front of the cabins, but guests can park there to drop off their luggage. Guest parking is in the remote dirt parking lot, which is not striped.

Cabin 19 is the accessible cabin. It features ramp access up to the front porch, a wide doorway and wood floors. It is furnished with a 27-inch high double bed with wheelchair-access on one side, and a 27-inch high twin bed in an alcove.

The bathroom has a wide pocket door and a full five-foot turning radius. It's equipped with a 35-inch deep roll-in shower with a 35-inch doorway. Other access features include a hand-held showerhead,

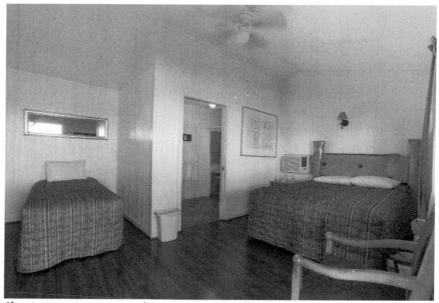

Sleeping area in western cabin 19 at Haulapai Ranch

Bathroom in western cabin 19 at Haulapai Ranch

Western cabin 19 at Haulapai Ranch

shower grab bars and a portable shower chair. The toilet grab bars are located on the right and back walls (as seated), and a lowered mirror is located above the pedestal sink.

There is a large bench on the front porch, with plenty of room to maneuver a wheelchair around it. A fire circle is located nearby, where the resident cowboys make s'mores and entertain guests in the evenings.

Breakfast is included in the room rate. It is served in the dining room and consists of scrambled eggs, sausage, fruit, toast and hot or cold beverages. All in all, the folks at Hualapai Ranch are very accommodating, and will do whatever they can to make your stay more enjoyable.

Resources

Reservations and Information

(888) 868-9378
www.hualapaitourism.com

Peach Springs

Also located on Hualapai land, Peach Springs is the gateway to a little-known driving route down to the Colorado River, at the bottom of the Grand Canyon. It's the perfect option for folks who can't manage the steep hike or mule ride down to Phantom Ranch from the South Rim. Accessible lodging is also available in Peach Springs, which is about three hours from Grand Canyon West. As an added bonus, this historic town is located along an original stretch of Route 66, halfway between Flagstaff and Kingman.

Attractions

Hualapai Cultural Center

Built on the site of the Qumacho Cafe, the Hualapai Cultural Center is the newest building in town. Open Monday through Friday, the center serves to preserve and promote Hualapai culture, through public education and cultural programs. Accessible parking is available on a concrete slab to the far left of the building, with level access to the front door. Inside, there is barrier-free access to all areas with

Hualapai Cultural Center

plenty of room to navigate a wheelchair. Although there's no formal tour, the receptionist is happy to show visitors around and answer questions. The cultural center features a nice collection of native artwork, as well as baskets, pottery and other items created by the young people of the tribe.

Peach Springs Trading Post and Gas Station

The historic Peach Springs Trading Post and Gas Station is located next door to the Hualapai Cultural Center. Built in the late 1920s by Ancel Taylor, it did a robust business during the heyday of Route 66. Sadly when the Mother Road was decommissioned, business died off until eventually the trading post and gas station were closed. The building was placed on the National Register of Historic Places in 2003. Today there are plaques commemorating the former business, but it is not open to the public. Still, it's interesting to have a look at the architecture and even peek inside the building. There is level access around the building, with plenty of room for wheelchair-users and slow walkers to navigate.

Diamond Creek Road

Peach Springs is also the gateway to the 19.5-mile driving route to the bottom of the Grand Canyon. It's an excellent choice for wheelchair-users and slow walkers, as you can get some great windshield views from the comfort of your own vehicle. A permit, which is required to drive the bottom of the canyon, can be purchased at Hualapai Lodge. A package deal that includes overnight lodging, a picnic lunch and a driving permit is also available.

The drive begins just across the street from Hualapai Lodge, as it winds through a residential area on a paved road. About a mile down the road, the pavement gives way to a graded dirt road. Although you don't need a four-wheel-drive vehicle to make the drive, it's not recommended for low clearance vehicles, as it gets rougher as you get closer to the river. Along the way you'll pass Diamond Peak, and as you descend, you'll notice a marked change of landscape; from juniper in the upper reaches to cactus down near the river. Shaded picnic tables are located about a mile from the river. Depending on weather conditions, the last stretch of the road may not be passable in a vehicle. There are also a couple of picnic tables on the beach, but even if you don't make it that far, it's still a beautiful drive. If you visit from April to September, you'll probably share the beach with some rafters, but during the rest of the year you'll most likely have it to yourself.

Lodging

Located on the south side of Route 66 between mile markers 103 and 104, Hualapai Lodge retains the flavor of yesteryear, but offers modern day amenities. There's accessible parking in front, with level access to the building. The lobby boasts a cozy river rock fireplace, and the walls are adorned with Hualapai artwork.

Accessible Room 117 is located just off the lobby. This extra-large room features wide doorways and good pathway access, and it's furnished with two 25-inch high double beds, with wheelchair access on both sides. The furnishings are rounded out with an easy chair, a desk and a chest of drawers.

Hualipai Lodge

Guestroom 117 at the Hualipai Lodge

The bathroom features a wide doorway and is equipped with a roll-in shower with a hand-held showerhead and a fold-down shower bench. Toilet grab bars are located on the back and left walls (as seated), and a roll-under sink is located in an alcove just outside the bathroom.

The room is located near the pool and spa area, which features barrier-free access. A pool lift is also provided.

Room 116 is also wheelchair accessible, but it's located closer to the railroad tracks. Room 117 faces the street and it is much quieter.

There is level access to the Diamond Creek Restaurant, located just down the hall from the lobby. The menu features Native American specialties, as well as American favorites. A Continental breakfast in the restaurant is included with the room rate. Alternatively, you can upgrade to a full breakfast for $5.

Entertainment by the fireplace is also offered during the high season. It's a very comfortable, clean and affordable property.

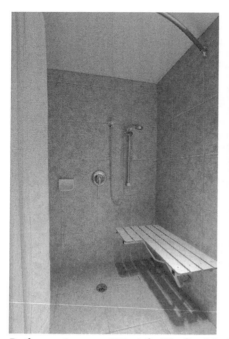

Bathroom in room 117 at the Hualipai Lodge

Resources

···

Reservations and Information

(888) 868-9378
www.hualapaitourism.com

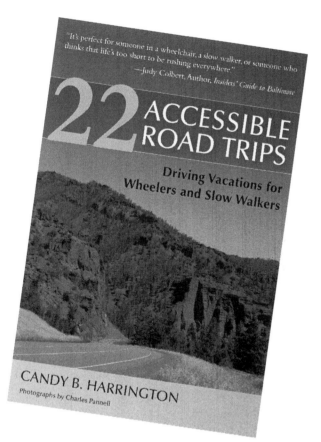

22 Accessible Road Trips
Driving Vacations for Wheelers and Slow Walkers

By Candy B. Harrington

Billed as the world's first inclusive road trip book, this detailed resource features 22 driving routes across the United States, with information about wheelchair-accessible sites, lodging options, trails, attractions and restaurants along the way. A great read for anyone who wants to hit the road — disabled or able-bodied — *22 Accessible Road Trips* captures the diversity of America, with off-the-beaten-path finds and unique roadside attractions, as well as must-see metropolitan sights in the gateway cities.

www.22AccessibleRoadTrips.com

Made in the USA
Middletown, DE
11 March 2015